Soar, My Butterfly
The Animal Dying Experience

By Gail Pope
President & Founder, BrightHaven

Cover Art: Blanca Walker
Editing, Layout & Design: Carol Howe Hulse & Kate Fenton

Disclaimer

I am not a veterinarian and therefore not qualified to give you professional veterinary advice. Always consult your family veterinarian in matters concerning the health of your animals.

I have, however, been helping our BrightHaven animals holistically since 1990, aided by many talented professional practitioners, and so I speak to you from our experiences along the way.

Proceeds from the sale of this booklet will help BrightHaven to assist more senior, chronically ill and disabled animals.

Soar, My Butterfly:
The Animal Dying Experience
Copyright 2015
ISBN:1517372984
All rights reserved.
Printed in the United States of America
No part of this booklet may be reproduced or transmitted in any form or by any means without prior written permission.

BrightHaven Inc.
P.O. Box 1743
Sebastopol, CA 95473-1743
www.brighthaven.org
707 578 4800

BrightHaven is a holistic animal sanctuary, hospice, rescue and education center and nonprofit organization.

Since 1990, BrightHaven has evolved into a unique hospice organization for over 600 senior, chronically ill and disabled animals, a population with an overwhelming need to find love and care in our society and most especially during the last phase of their lives.

BrightHaven hospice care is modeled on human hospice care. When an animal enters hospice care our expectation is that the animal will have a painless, loving, peaceful journey followed by a painless, loving, peaceful and natural death.

Our BrightHaven mission is one of healing for body, mind and spirit for our animal family. We seek healing for their highest good rather than a cure and firmly believe that in order to have a "good death," one must prepare or set the stage for that to happen. I have written about that in my last book, *The BrightHaven Guide to Animal Hospice*, available at www.smile.amazon.com.

BrightHaven also offers an animal hospice online learning program. For more information please visit www.brighthaven.org/education.

To learn more about BrightHaven, please visit www.brighthaven.org.

Letting Go

A joyous rebirth—
New adventures await you.
Soar, my butterfly.

By Carol Howe Hulse
BrightHaven Education Program Specialist

This booklet is dedicated, with love and appreciation:

- ❖ to all of the wonderful animals who helped me gather this knowledge by sharing their deaths, and

- ❖ to Barbara Karnes, whose extremely helpful work about the human dying experience entitled *Gone from my Sight* inspired me to share my knowledge about the animal dying experience.

Table of Contents

Introduction 1
Supportive Tips 2
Pain Control 3
Fear 3
Animal Reiki 3
Part 1: 1–3 months prior to death 5
Part 2: 1–2 weeks prior to death 9
Starvation at End of Life 9
Dehydration at End of Life 9
Part 3: A Few Days to Hours Prior to Death 19
Part 4: The Moment of Death 27
Summary of Timing 29
Different Types of Death: the BrightHaven Perspective 31
The Slow and Easy (the animal is aware of surrounings) 31
The Big Easy (the animal is not aware of surroundings) 31
The Fast Track 31
The Restless and Frustrating 31
After Death 32
Conclusion 33
Suggested Resources 35
Hospice Websites 35
Authors 35
My Mentors 37

Introduction

I created this booklet to provide both knowledge and comfort to those who are accompanying a beloved animal companion on the journey to transition. It is written as a simple guide to the signs and symptoms that you may encounter during the final stages of actual dying--a process that may begin several months before death finally occurs.

I will share with you, in brief form, the meaning of what you see, as well as what you can do to help your animal friend when you confront these various signs and symptoms.

No two deaths are ever exactly the same as each being approaches and experiences death in his or her own unique way. There are no exact rules and nothing is set in stone. One animal may follow a certain pattern and timeline to death and another will have a very different experience, so please remember that this booklet can only serve as a guide to what you might expect to see and when it might happen.

Since 1990 I have learned about animal care from many wise people. In the early years of BrightHaven I worked for three years for Douglas Coward, DVM. Doug became BrightHaven's first supervising veterinarian and to this day remains my mentor and good friend. Our current veterinarian, Christine Barrett, DVM has been providing her generous support for more than a decade and is always available for advice and information regarding both the conventional and holistic paths.

My knowledge of animal hospice care has primarily been learned from more than 600 animals who I have cared for through the end of their lives. During that experience I was fortunate to meet Dr. Ella Bittel, whose passion for animal hospice care became fuel for my own passion, which continues to grow. Ella taught me much about both human and animal hospice care and their similarities. When I cared for my own mother at home in hospice care for six months everything fell into place and I truly realized that dying is a process and very much the same for humans and animals.

I was honored to be a founding board member for the International Association for Animal Hospice and Palliative Care (IAAHPC) when founder Amir Shanan, DVM became my good friend and another mentor. Barbara Karnes, RN is a renowned end of life nurse and hospice educator and when I read her informative and wonderfully inspiring booklet *Gone from my Sight*, I immediately thought how much a similar booklet for animal caregivers could be of value. When contacted, Barbara agreed with alacrity and so helped me give birth to this booklet.

Supportive Tips

Here are a few tips I have learned along the way that may help you through this challenging time.

- Effective hospice care requires a team approach. Your team includes your veterinarian, **conventional and/or holistic**. It may also include other healthcare practitioners, a veterinary technician, a grief counselor or a spiritual support person and relatives or friends to offer respite care.

- Healing (balancing of body, mind and spirit) can be achieved without a cure (absence of symptoms).

- Death is a process as is birth.

- Approaching death can most often be peaceful; the difficult, unpleasant things that may (or may not) happen generally, occur as part of living before the dying process begins or in its early stages, and can be treated accordingly by your veterinarian.

- Self-care is very important. Rest and remember that you are doing the very best you can for your beloved animal friend. Trust in the process and allow the situation to direct your actions.

- If you hear yourself saying, "I can't stand to see my animal this way!" be gentle with yourself, know you are doing your best and be sure to address pain control with your veterinarian at all stages during hospice care and the dying process.

- Your intuition is your ally—listen to it.

- The power of love and being present is amazing!

Pain Control

When hospice care commences it is of paramount and ongoing importance for caregivers to proactively discuss pain control with their veterinarian. Many species of animals have evolved to hide signs of pain, and therefore one should be extra vigilant for any signs of pain.

Fear

Fear is a natural emotion. Fear and courage are factors for the companion on the journey, particularly if you have not experienced a natural passing before, either human or animal, for there really is little difference if they are hospice-assisted. It can greatly help to keep remembering that death is a process, most often spread over many months and above all that it is not due to a failed medical event. It's important to learn about and embrace death as part of the circle of life. With birth, it **IS** the most natural thing in life and happens to us all.

Animal Reiki

Since Kathleen Prasad of Animal Reiki Source introduced animal Reiki to BrightHaven in 2004, this gentle, healing practice has become an integral part of BrightHaven daily life.

What is animal Reiki? It's essentially meditating with your animals. But in a broader sense, Reiki is a spiritual system cultivating compassionate intention, which in turn may bring about healing transformation. The practices of Reiki help us navigate life's challenges with grace and surrender while we to learn to listen to and be present for others in a compassionate space: offering one's self as a conduit through which energy can flow for the good of another is the single most powerful gift that one can give and receive.

I've discovered that perhaps the most important benefit of Reiki comes towards the end of life, at a time when there is nothing left to do but await transition. It is at this time when humans often feel completely ineffective and wish they could do more, or be a part of the journey in a more helpful, meaningful way.

Now we can. To offer Reiki during a beloved animal's transition and the days or weeks beforehand is to feel something miraculous taking place, as Reiki offers healing, peace and bliss to all involved. Here at BrightHaven we have long held the belief that healing is needed for wellness and also for transition to the next life, and we see just that as we offer Reiki.

"Easy for anyone to learn and use, Reiki can do no harm, even when used by the most novice practitioner. It always goes to the deepest source of the problem and always supports a path towards balance and harmony."
—Kathleen Prasad, *Animal Reiki Source*

For more information on animal Reiki, please visit **www.animalreiki-source.com**.

Part 1: 1–3 Months Prior to Death

We believe that the animal knows the dying process has begun; this is often a period of gradual withdrawal from normal daily life.

Please note: *This booklet is purely intended as reference for the companion/caregiver and does not purport to give any medical advice. These guidelines are written on the assumption that the caregiver is consulting with their own veterinarian. Any sign of pain should be addressed immediately with your veterinarian.*

Emotional and Behavioral Changes		
What you may see	Desccription	What you can do
Withdrawal	Seeking solitude; withdrawal from social interaction. Seeking more affection.	Speak and touch gently and reassuringly. Play soothing music. Never startle the animal with bright lights. Always identify yourself. You may not be recognized at this time. Allow time for silence. Dying requires energy and focus. Try not to distract the animal from this necessary preparation. Remember that you are supporting the animal to "let go."
Sleeping more than usual	More periods of rest, sleeping and lethargy	Be supportive and present. Refrain from trying to bring the animal back to reality. Sometimes apparently bad dreams can be caused by medications or metabolic changes.

Physical Changes		
Organ system	What you may see	What you can do
Digestive System	Decreased food and water intake.	Be proactive in trying different foods, textures and feeding methods but do not become overbearing and never force-feed a dying animal. If a small amount of food (perhaps pureed) is placed in the animal's mouth and s/he swallows easily and does not seem to mind, then try a little more. The animal will tell you when to stop. Depending upon the illness it may be sensible to discuss a feeding tube with your veterinarian, although if the dying process has begun, then a tube may result more in discomfort rather than the intended added comfort from improved nutritional status.
Muscular and Skeletal System	Muscle weakness and gradual weight loss.	This is normal.

Integumentary System: Skin	Dehydration. The classic sign of dehydration is skin tenting: If you take a pinch of skin over the shoulders and pull up gently, the skin should snap back into place when released. Other signs that may be noted include: dry, tacky gums, listlessness, refusal to eat.	Subcutaneous fluid therapy can be very helpful in the early stages of dying as recommended by your veterinarian.

Part 2: 1–2 Weeks Prior to Death

The animal's focus may begin shifting from this life to the next during this time period.

Please note: *This booklet is purely intended as reference for the companion/caregiver and does not purport to give any medical advice. These guidelines are written on the assumption that you are consulting with your veterinarian. Any sign of pain in your animal should be immediately addressed with your veterinarian.*

Starvation at End of Life

It is a common and widespread fear that an animal who stops eating will die of starvation. As we know, dying is a gradual process, often taking place over months, and a key part of the natural way to die involves food. Food keeps our body alive, keeps us grounded and gives us energy. I think of my body as the vehicle I drive through life and food as the fuel that keeps it running.

As appetite decreases and food becomes less appealing, we should initially become innovative in our ideas to tempt the palate, but also be watchful for the time when eating stops, as it should.

This is perhaps the most difficult time for humans to bear. In our modern society we equate food with the expression of love, but must realize that the body no longer needs or wishes for food as it can no longer process it into energy. Life is ebbing away and death is coming. Food is no longer necessary or helpful.

Lack of food also has the benefit of increased production of endorphins in the brain, chemicals that promote comfort and restfulness and act as natural pain relief.

Dehydration at End of Life

If you need help in interpreting physical changes or are ever unsure of what to do, please contact your veterinarian immediately.

Dehydration can be uncomfortable and we often see our patients feeling better with subcutaneous fluids, especially in the early stages of hospice care. Thus we do continue to offer fluids in decreasing amounts right to the end of life, or for as long as the body tissues can absorb them.

It's important to be able to recognize when fluids are no longer being absorbed: when this happens, fluids may migrate from the shoulders to hang underneath the armpits or flow down to the paws. You will see and feel distinct swelling and puffiness as edema develops. In this event fluid therapy should be discontinued to prevent additional discomfort.

Many people are surprised to learn that the natural process of dehydration at the end of life does have a positive effect on the dying process. As illness progresses, the body's systems slow down and dehydration is nature's way of regulating fluids so that the circulatory system is not overloaded. Another benefit of dehydration, as with lack of food, is the body's release of endorphins, chemicals that produce natural pain relief.

On the other hand, we have often experienced last-minute turnarounds in BrightHaven animals close to the end of life, and so are very careful to continue support with fluid therapy, but in reducing amounts. We watch carefully so that we know when to stop, to allow nature's process to continue unhindered.

Be aware, also, that too many fluids can cause other problems, especially if the heart is failing. Additional strain on the heart may result in breathing difficulty or a potassium deficiency.

Again, if you need help in interpreting physical changes or are ever unsure of what to do, please contact your veterinarian immediately.

Behavioral and Emotional Changes		
What you may see	Description	What you can do
Disorientation	The animal seems to be living almost in two worlds now, almost as though s/he has a foot on each side.	Be gentle, kind and supportive.
Sleeping more and more	The animal is sleeping more but can still easily be aroused.	Allow the sleeping periods to be undisturbed; be supportive. Assume that everything you say can be heard, as the sense of hearing is thought to persist, even when the human or animal is unconscious, in a coma or otherwise not responsive.
Confusion	The animal may act strangely, sometimes as though you or familiar things or places are not recognized.	Be gentle, kind and supportive. Speak to the animal softly, and identify yourself when you approach.

Behavioral and Emotional Changes		
What you may see	Description	What you can do
Agitation and restlessness	Unable to settle peacefully.

Pacing or wandering from room to room.

Restless and changing position often in bed.

Anxious or in a state of nervous excitement some of the time. | This is very normal in the dying process but please seek advice from your veterinarian in case pain is present and requires treatment.

Consider the animal has unresolved business—do you need to give them permission to die or tell them you will be OK? |

Physical Changes		
Organ system	What you may see	What you can do
Digestive System: Appetite	Appetite diminishing (anorexia).

Animals may eat dirt and also lick rocks or concrete, perhaps seeking minerals (pica). | Continue to be proactive in trying different foods, textures and feeding methods but never force-feed a dying animal.

It is best to offer very small amounts (drops from a syringe) and observe the throat to be sure swallowing has taken place. Tolerance of food generally progresses from solid to soft to liquids and then only small amounts of water. In the very last stages of life the animal probably won't want any food or drink. |

Thirst	Thirst diminishing or increasing (polydipsia)--cats may show a tendency to sit or lie beside their water bowls but not drink. Cats may also be seen lying in their litter box for extended periods.

Some cats and dogs may show a desire to drink dirty water from puddles in the garden, perhaps seeking minerals. | Be sure water is fresh.

It may help to add liquid minerals to drinking water. |
Mouth	With the decrease in peripheral circulation, the lips and gums become pale grey, bluish or white, and cooler to the touch.	Be supportive and if in doubt please contact your veterinarian.
Muscular and Skeletal System	Exhaustion--body seems tired and heavy.	Be gentle, kind and supportive. Encourage rest.
	Increasing weight loss with loss of muscle mass causing stiffness.	This is normal, but be aware that stiffness can also be an indicator of pain.
	Extremities (lower legs, paws ears and tail) noticeably cooler.	This is also very normal and gentle massage may be of help.
Nervous System: Eyes	Eyes may start to lose their gleam and look dull.	Nothing essential. Gentle eye drops can be used if dryness is present.

Physical Changes

Organ system	What you may see	What you can do
Integumentary System: **Skin**	Continuing dehydration. Be on the lookout for edema. (puffiness or swelling which may develop due to the body's inability to process fluid as the heart weakens).	Subcutaneous fluid therapy can be very helpful in the early stages of dying as recommended by your veterinarian. One also should keep in mind that last-minute turnarounds do occur in animals appearing close to the end of life, warranting the utmost caution in making the decision to discontinue fluid therapy altogether. Please discuss this issue with your veterinarian, who may recommend gradually decreasing the amounts of daily fluid administered while monitoring your animal closely for signs of edema.

Skin (cont.)	Hot or cold or sweating or excessive itching	At this time it's best to follow the wishes of the dying animal to maintain comfort even if it's against reason--like not trying to keep them covered when they keep kicking the blankets off. To cool: Use damp, cool washcloth or a cool compress to the forehead and pulse areas. Use a small electric fan placed near the bed if they feel really hot. To warm: Place a warm blanket gently over them. In earlier stages a heating pad may have proven useful but now great care is needed to not overheat the animal who cannot move away. Avoid drafts that may cause the body's temperature to fall quickly and cause shivering. Change any soiled bed linen. This is a good opportunity to give a gentle massage and reposition the animal comfortably. Try to keep the animal as comfortable as possible.
	Skin may become noticeably pale or bluish in color due to the tissues near the skin surface having low oxygen saturation (hypoxemia)—mostly in rear legs.	Normally, repositioning the animal is advised every few hours, but when close to death it is not necessary to turn for circulation. Changing the animal's position is only necessary if it helps breathing or provides more comfort. Always observe how well the animal settles into a new position and if s/he's not comfortable, try another position, or gently return the animal to the previous position, and consider pain relief.

Physical Changes		
Organ system	What you may see	What you can do
Integumentary System: Skin (cont.)	Wound healing may be prolonged or absent.	Keep affected areas clean and use products like Manuka honey or MSM cream if necessary on wounds. To protect wounds from flies use mosquito netting.
	Flea problems, if previously present during chronic illness, will intensify at end ol life and remain for a short period after death. (Fleas are attracted by a weak immune system.)	Flea comb frequently or use another holistic approach to bring relief, and ensure bedding is changed often.
Urinary/Excretory System: Bowel and bladder function	Incontinence (bladder and/or bowels). Constipation. The need to urinate frequently (polyuria). Dark, concentrated (hematuria) or colorless, dilute urine.	Watch for signs of constipation and treat if necessary, perhaps via a gentle warm water enema or manual expression as directed by your veterinarian. Signs of irritability or grumpiness can sometimes be an indicator of constipation or pain. Layer bed-clothes with waterproofing sheeting (various kinds available) to facilitate bed changing. Consider layering different areas, e.g. under mouth as well as rear end. We have great success in using homeopathy and other holistic modalities where there are obvious symptoms to be treated

Respiratory System: Breathing and congestion	Respiration irregular with some puffing and blowing of the lips on exhalation, congestion, coughing, snapping at imaginary flies (fly catcher's syndrome), panting—all symptoms coming and going.	Respiratory issues can increase any fear that may already be present for either the animal or the caregiver. They are normal and not cause for panic. If in bed, raise the animal's head or the head of the bed to help breathing. If secretions are pooling in the mouth, turn the head and position the body so that gravity can drain them. If appropriate, wipe out the mouth with a soft, moist cloth to cleanse excess secretions. Speak gently and lovingly, and use gentle reassuring touch to ease fear.
Circulatory System: Blood pressure	Fluctuations in blood pressure: High (hypertension) or Low (hypotension)	As with humans, some animals may have high or low blood pressure during the dying process. This may have been previously diagnosed in chronic illness. There would be no obvious symptoms. If in doubt please call your veterinarian for advice.
Heartbeat, pulse	Heart and circulation failing: Slow heart beat (brachycardia) Fast heart beat (tachycardia) Pulses variable	Be present, calm and peaceful and if in doubt please contact your veterinarian.

Physical Changes		
Organ system	What you may see	What you can do
Other	Growing odor, which may become putrid (emanating from end stage renal failure as well as some cancers).	A room spray of lavender or other essential oils may help.

Part 3: A Few Days to Hours Prior to Death

This period may herald a swan song, which is a metaphorical phrase for a final gesture, effort or performance given just before death. The phrase refers to an ancient belief that swans sing a beautiful song just before death, having been silent previously.

Your animal may become more affectionate, active, hungry or thirsty again. In other words, s/he may appear to suddenly be improving as though coming back to life again. Some do, most do not; please enjoy this very special time.

After the swan song may likely come the time of the vigil when there is little to do but to be simply present in love and the moment with your animal friend. Reiki is particularly helpful at this time on through transition.

Please note: *This booklet is purely intended as reference for the companion/caregiver and does not purport to give any medical advice. These guidelines are written on the assumption that you are consulting with your veterinarian. Any sign of pain in your animal should be immediately addressed with your veterinarian.*

Behavioral and Emotional Changes		
What you may see	Description	What you can do
Personality	Blank stare, departure from normal personality, or very present and affectionate.	Speak and touch gently and reassuringly. Play soothing music. Never startle the animal with bright lights. Always identify yourself. You may not be recognized at this time. Allow time for silence. Dying requires energy and focus. Try not to distract the dying one from this necessary preparation. Remember that you are supporting the animal to "let go."
Rest and sleep	Drowsiness, loss of consciousness or stepping in and out of body at times (other worldly).	Be supportive and present. Refrain from trying to bring the animal back to reality. Sometimes apparently bad dreams can be caused by medications or metabolic changes.
Agitation	Restlessness can increase due to lack of oxygen in the blood.	This is very normal in the dying process but do not hesitate to seek veterinary advice if necessary. Consider the animal has unresolved business—do you need to give them permission to die or tell them you will be OK?

Agitation (cont.)	Moaning, groaning, grimacing (terminal delirium)	Terminal delirium is sometimes wrongly diagnosed as pain. Please be sure to discuss this with your veterinarian.
Stillness	Collapsed/ peaceful	A time to simply be present and in the moment with and for your loved one.

Physical Changes		
Organ System	**What you may see**	**What you can do**
Digestive System: Food and water intake	Generally not taking any food or water by mouth.	It may be comforting to a dying animal to offer drops of water to the side of the mouth by syringe (check swallowing ability first). You can moisten the lips and mouth with a small amount of water or a sponge-tipped applicator dipped in water. Protect lips and nose from dryness with a protective balm like a non-petroleum jelly preparation. Continue to be a caring and loving presence.

Physical Changes		
Organ System	What you may see	What you can do
Mouth	Tissue mostly white. Thick, sticky, stringy mucus (phlegm) can accumulate.	Try to allow the phlegm to drain naturally by turning the head and cleaning with a tissue. You may be able to remove a little by using an oral care swab.
Swallowing	The ability to swallow (dysphagia) may be lost.	Forcing fluid may cause choking, or liquid may be drawn into the lungs. Refrain from giving liquids unless the animal is obviously willing and able to accept them.
Muscular and Skeletal System	Muscle spasms/ twitching (myoclonus).	This is a normal part of the dying process and a time to be present and calm and if in doubt contact your veterinarian.
Legs and extremities: Temperature	Extremities, including front legs, cold with loss of sensation.	At this time it's best to follow the wishes of the dying animal to maintain comfort even if it's against reason--like not trying to keep them covered when they keep kicking the blankets off. Animals have a built in knowing that the body needs to cool in order to die. Many will seek a cool floor or the earth outdoors. They may well also prefer a darkened place, to simulate being under a bush in nature. Try to keep the animal as comfortable as possible.

Legs: Skin color	Due to decreased blood perfusion both front and back legs may be purplish in color (cyanosis) and blotchy.	A time to be present and calm and if in doubt contact your veterinarian. Be supportive and perhaps a little gentle massage may help.
The jaw	Slow, repetitive motions may continue as if to indicate an unpleasant taste or jaws may remain slightly open or mouth may be closed.	A time to be present and calm and if in doubt contact your veterinarian. Remember to keep talking. You will be heard.
Nervous System	Eyes may now be open or semi-open and unseeing. They may also be glassy and wet or dry.	Nothing essential, although eye drops may ease very dry eyes.
Integumentary System: Skin	End stage dehydration will most likely be present with the skin stretched very tight.	Subcutaneous fluid therapy will most likely have been discontinued at this stage.

Physical Changes		
Organ System	What you may see	What you can do
Integumentary System: Skin (cont.)	Wounds heal, masses shrink/ discharges dry.	Continue to protect the animal from flies.
	Flea problems, if previously present during chronic illness, will intensify at end of life and remain for a short period after death. (Fleas are attracted by a weak immune system.)	Flea comb frequently or use another holistic approach to bring relief, and ensure bedding is changed often.
Urinary/Excretory System: Bladder function	Thicker and darker urine with failure of the kidneys to make urine (anuria), or very dilute urine.	Ensure bed is well protected with layers of waterproof pads and absorbent towels.
Bowel function	No stool generally or a little black, tarry diarrhea (melena).	Gentle, non-invasive clean up where necessary.

Respiratory System: Breathing	Accumulation of respiratory secretions ("death rattle"). Cheyne-Stokes respiration (a loud, deep inhalation followed by a pause of not breathing (apnea), before a loud, deep breath resumes and again slowly peters out). Agonal breathing (gasping, "fish out of water" breathing), sometimes with vocalizing and twitching of muscles (myoclonus). Breathing may only be visible by the gently rising and falling of the abdomen.	These different breathing patterns are very normal, although sometimes scary to the caregiver.
Congestion	Can be loud and comes and goes. Phlegm can accumulate in the mouth.	Congestion can often be relieved by turning the animal and allowing phlegm to drain more easily.
Circulatory System: Blood pressure	Blood pressure dropping. There will be no obvious symptoms.	Be supportive, present and peaceful and if in doubt call your veterinarian for advice.

Physical Changes		
Organ System	What you may see	What you can do
Circulatory System (cont.): Heartbeat and circulation	Irregular heartbeat and no circulation.	Be supportive, present and peaceful and if in doubt call your veterinarian for advice.
Other	Odor, which may now be putrid.	You may continue the use of a diluted lavender or other essential oils room spray.

Part 4: The Moment of Death

We have reached the last minutes of life and at this stage the animal is now most likely unresponsive, although some remain present to the very last breath.

Coping with this last phase of life can largely depend upon how an individual views death and that individual's fears about the subject. For some it is simply like stepping out of an old suit of clothes that no longer fits and for others, death marks the end of everything.

Please note: *This booklet is purely intended as reference for the companion/caregiver and does not purport to give any medical advice. These guidelines are written on the assumption that you are consulting with your veterinarian. Any sign of pain in your animal should be immediately addressed with your veterinarian.*

What you may see	Clinical death definition	What you can do
Fish out of water and agonal breathing characterized by spasmodic jerky contractions of muscles (myoclonus) and stretching out slowly of front and rear limbs while head tilts backwards. One final small gasp or sigh.	Cessation of breathing.	Support the body and neck gently to allow the animal to lean backwards and fully stretch out.
Heart arrest and no circulation.	Cardiac arrest--cessation of heartbeat.	Be present, calm and peaceful.

What you may see	Clinical death definition	What you can do
Dramatic drop in blood pressure.	Cessation of blood circulation.	Be present, calm and peaceful.
Fixed and dilated pupils. Sometimes release of bowel or bladder.		Be present, calm and peaceful. Be prepared with waterproof sheet underneath.

"There are many similarities between labour pains of dying and those of being born. It is the same doorway; all are passing through, some coming in and others going out.

"On either side of the doorway midwives are needed to guide this passage. Both are a holy service requiring a great work of labour and love. Both are moments of vulnerability and the same preparation that is encouraged for birth is also as valuable for death. Through this preparation and deeper understanding of the deathing process it is possible for pain to exist and be lessened by tenderness, love and compassion.

"Death can be a long labouring process, and, again as in birthing, gentle touching, massaging, words of encouragement to relax and let go, gentle singing and cradling are all greatly comforting. A midwife knows how to practice inner stillness and be peacefully present putting aside any pains or sorrows. The midwife tenderly holds the energy, keeps vigil and guards the almost invisible gossamer film of light while the dying person passes through the matrix.

"This transition leaves in its wake a divine stillness which touches the very depths of the soul, leaving a feeling of the presence of the miraculous and the mysterious."

—Wendy Hayhurst
Certified Soul Midwife

Summary of Timing of Changes Preceding Death

Some, all or none of the symptoms may be present.

1–3 months:

Behavioral and emotional ehanges
Withdrawal, more time alone and sleeping more or seeking more affection

Physical changes
Gradual decrease in appetite
Gradual weight and muscle mass loss
Dehydration

1–2 weeks:

Behavioral and emotional changes
Disorientation–seeming quite often to be in two worlds
Sleeping more & more deeply; still responsive
Confusion–focus changing
Agitation

Physical changes
Appetite diminishing and drinking less
Mouth: Lips and gums paler and cooler
Cats often seek water; lie beside the bowl
Cats may also lie in their litter box
Increasing weight and muscle mass loss
Eyes becoming dull
Dehydration increasing
Body temperature, hot or cold and sweating
Body tired, heavy with exhaustion
Legs: skin color paler, bluish and cooler
Wound healing prolonged or absent
Incontinence/constipation
Urine output increased or decreased
Breathing changes respiration irregular; puffing and blowing of the lips on exhalation, congestion, coughing—all coming and going
Blood pressure decreased
Pulses variable
Growing odor

A few days or hours:

Behavioral and emotional changes
Surge of energy known as a swan song
May become unresponsive to environment and others
Restlessness and anxiety—or no activity at all

Physical changes
Many symptoms of past 1-2 weeks intensify
Little or no food or water
Swallowing difficult
Mouth tissue almost white/thick phlegm
Slow repetitive jaw motion
Muscle spasms and twitching anywhere in the body
Eyes become glassy or fixed, half open; can be wet with mucous, or drying
Dehydration more severe
Extremities cold and becoming purplish with loss of sensation
Wounds appear to be healing
Decreased urine output--concentrated
Increased urine output--very dilute
Incontinence of bladder and/or bowels
Breathing patterns slower and more irregular and sometimes even stop awhile; abdominal breathing
Congestion louder—death rattle
Blood pressure dropping
Pulses weak and irregular
Irregular heartbeat
Odor stronger

Minutes:
Unresponsive, but can remain present
Fish out of water breathing, agonal breathing
Jaw may be open or closed
Stretching out of limbs—back then front
Gasping
Fixed and dilated pupils
Bladder or bowels release
No heartbeat; body becomes limp

The Different Types of Death: the BrightHaven Perspective

The Slow and Easy (the animal is aware of surroundings)
This type is, in my opinion, the best kind of natural dying process. There is contact and communication all the way to the very end, a very precious time when the caregiver is able to hold the animal's paws, gaze into each other's eyes, and talk of many things. Some animals will remain in eye and finger contact as they draw their last breath, an extremely reassuring, comforting and beautiful experience.

The Big Easy (the animal is not aware of surroundings)
There is mostly peace and calm, sometimes for days on end as the animal slips back and forth between worlds and between degrees of unconsciousness. The last, almost imperceptible breath slips away with grace and tenderness.

The Fast Track
…is exactly that. The animal seems set to live a while longer, but then suddenly experiences physical changes that lead to death in a matter of seconds or a few minutes.

The Restless and Frustrating
This type is seen in approximately 5% of human hospice patients and referred to sometimes as "the difficult road to death." These deaths generally involve terminal delirium as defined in human hospice. BrightHaven sees this type of death in less than 1% of our animals.

After Death

Honoring the departed is important, not only for your loved one but also for your own grieving process. These processes will be different depending on one's religious or spiritual views, and so I offer here a glimpse into our BrightHaven way: as we honor each of our residents in death, we also celebrate their lives and our wonderful memories. The death of any being can be a profound lesson for us all.

With each passing, we grow stronger in our belief that by allowing our residents to complete the journey, with dignity and on their terms, we honor them in a special way, and that extends to the care of their body after the last breath has been taken.

As discussed in spiritual writings and also scientifically documented, we have learned that at least three days are needed for life energy to fully depart the body after physical death. These three days have become a special time at BrightHaven as we conduct our rituals of preparing the body, sharing memories and allowing visitations and viewings. The body lies in state under a favorite coverlet surrounded by candles, flowers and mementos for a three-day period while friends, family and volunteers pay their respects and bid farewell, not unlike the process offered after the death of a human family member.

Conclusion

Please accept my sincere appreciation for reading Soar, My *Butterfly*. I hope you found it informative, helpful and perhaps inspiring.

If you are following a journey through the dying process with a beloved one at present, my heart goes out to you at this challenging yet very profound time. I have cared for more than 600 animals at the end of their lives since 1990 and they have taught me more than I can ever say about life and love and the circle of life. I've learned so much about living in the moment, acceptance, joy, heartache and sorrow. These experiences have, without a doubt, helped me to grow in so many ways.

Mostly I have learned that there is no greater gift in life than to be present during the hospice time as well as at the end of this beautiful journey, to share love with another, and most especially to do so with courage and grace.

With my love, blessings & gratitude,

Gail Pope

President & Founder, BrightHaven

Soar Away My Butterfly

Soar away my butterfly, carrying the light of my beloved one.
Your beautiful presence is leaving my side dissolving into particles of light.
I remember our playful days and nights when I enjoyed your gentle touch.
My eyes shed the sad tears of loss.

I remember how much you made me laugh and the joy you brought to my life.
I'll never forget the connection we made when our hearts became one and our souls intertwined.
I wipe my tears and wonder what you would have done were I the one to leave your side.

You would have not cried for what I feel as a loss.
You would have filled your heart with fond memories knowing there are no goodbyes, only a small pause.
You would have found joy and laughter as you lived in the moment and not in the past.

Oh my wise companion, you've taught me so much, to see beyond what meets the eye, to look deep inside myself
To honor nature and respect its path, to love with an open heart and never judge.
To truly enjoy and live each moment and cherish every day as though my last.

Today I saw you my butterfly, gliding proudly in the blue sky
There are no goodbyes – only a small pause
Soar away my butterfly, disappearing into the light, carrying the spirit of my beloved as I patiently wait
Until it's my time to fly.

This poem is dedicated to all those I've loved who have brought light to my life

By Blanca Walker
BrightHaven Animal Care Specialist

Suggested Resources

Hospice Websites

International Association of Animal Hospice and Palliative Care (IAAHPC): www.iaahpc.org

International Association of Animal Hospice and Palliative Care Guidelines: www.iaahpc.org/images/IAAHPCAnimalHospiceGuidelines2013.pdf

National Hospice and Palliative Care Organization: www.nhpco.org

Spirits in Transition: www.spiritsintransition.org

The Hospice Foundation of America: www.hospicefoundation.org

The Nikki Hospice Foundation: www.pethospice.org

Authors

Richard Bach
Avid aviator and author, touching on themes of flight and enlightenment.
Works include *Jonathan Livingston Seagull*; *Illusions*.

Gregg Braden
A blend of scientist, visionary & scholar.
Works include *The Divine Matrix*.

Richard F. Groves
Executive Director at Sacred Art of Living Center.
Works include *The American Book of Living and Dying*.

Thích Nhất Hạnh
Vietnamese Buddhist monk, teacher, author, poet and peace activist.
Works include *Being Peace, Moments of Mindfulness*.

Wendy Hayhurst
Certified Soul Midwife.
Works include *Coming for to Carry Me Home*.

Barbara Karnes, RN
End of life nurse and hospice educator.
Works include *Gone from my Sight*.

Dr. Konstantin G. Korotkov
Russian biophysicist, inventor, and pioneer in the scientific field called electrophotonics; invented the Gas Discharge Visualization, or GDV, technique by which the energy fields emanating from humans may be viewed in real time.
Works include *Light after Life*.

Elizabeth Kübler-Ross
Pioneer in near-death studies and celebrated author.
Works include *On Death and Dying*.

Bruce Lipton
A developmental biologist best known for promoting the idea that genes and DNA can be manipulated by a person's beliefs.
Works include *The Biology of Belief*.

Kathleen Prasad
Lifelong animal lover and educator.
Works include *The Animal Reiki Handbook*; *Reiki for Dogs*.

Sogyal Rinpoche
A Tibetan Dzogchen lama of the Nyingma tradition; the founder and spiritual director of Rigpa.
Works include *The Tibetan Book of Living and Dying*.

My Mentors

Vicki Allinson, holistic practitioner and animal communicator (deceased)

Christine Barrett, DVM

Douglas Coward, DVM
Animal and Bird Clinic of Mission Viejo
www.abcofmv.vetsuite.com/Templates/exotic.aspx

Jeff Levy, DVM, PCH
Homeovet
www.homeovet.net

Kathleen Prasad
Animal Reiki Source
www.animalreikisource.com

Amir Shanan, DVM
Compassionate Veterinary Hospice
www.pethospicechicago.com/veterinarian-hospice-chicago/dr-amir-shanan-dvm.php

Notes

Copyright 2015

This publication or any part of it may not be copied, photo-copied, translated, reprinted, reproduced, stored in or introduced into a retrieval system or transmitted in any form or by any means (electronic, mechanical, recording or otherwise) without the prior written permission of the author of this book. The scanning, uploading and distribution of this book via the internet or any other means without permission is illegal and punishable by law.

Your support of the author's rights is appreciated.

To order more copies visit www.amazon.com. If you purchase via www.smile.amazon.com and select BrightHaven as your favorite charitable organization, Amazon will donate a percentage of the purchase price to BrightHaven!

For information please contact:

BrightHaven Inc.
P.O. Box 1743
Sebastopol, CA 95473-1743
www.brighthaven.org
707 578 4800

Made in the USA
San Bernardino, CA
23 August 2018